eco GUIDES

A Teen Guide to

Eco-Fashion

Liz Gogerly

Raintree

Raintree is an imprint of Capstone Global Library Limited, a company incorporated in England and Wales having its registered office at 7 Pilgrim Street, London, EC4V 6LB – Registered company number: 6695582

To contact Raintree:
Phone: 0845 6044371
Fax: + 44 (0) 1865 312263
Email: myorders@raintreepublishers.co.uk
Outside the UK please telephone +44 1865 312262.

Edited by Andrew Farrow, Adam Miller, and Vaarunika Dharmapala
Designed by Richard Parker
Original illustrations © Capstone Global Library Ltd 2013
Illustrated by HL Studios
Picture research by Tracy Cummins
Originated by Capstone Global Library Ltd
Printed and bound in China by CTPS

ISBN 978 1 406 24984 2
16 15 14 13 12
10 9 8 7 6 5 4 3 2 1

British Library Cataloguing in Publication Data
Gogerly, Liz.
A teen guide to eco-fashion. -- (Eco guides)
746.9'2-dc23
A full catalogue record for this book is available from the British Library.

Acknowledgements
We would like to thank the following for permission to reproduce photographs: Alamy pp. 18 (© Stuart Kelly), 30 (© keith morris), 33 (top)(© NetPhotos), 42 (© Richard Green/Commercial); Capstone Library pp. 11, 25, 26, 27, 35, 36, 37 (Karon Dubke), 44; Corbis p. 22 (© DreamPictures/Blend Images); EU Ecolabel p. 20 (bottom left); Getty Images pp. 14 (Steven Puetzer), 15 (Lalage Snow/AFP), 19 (Maria Valentino/ FTWP), 23 (Howard Grey), 40 (LUIS ROBAYO/AFP), 45 (bottom) (Lambert/ Archive Photos), 46 (altrendo images); H&M Image p. 39; International Working Group on Global Organic Textile Standard p 20 (centre); istockphoto pp. 4 (© quavondo), 7 (© Ralph125), 13 (© Antonio Ciro Russo), 24 (© andipantz), 29 (© Brandy Taylor), 38 (© Alan Crawford); Newscom pp. 5 (Sergei Bachlakov/Xinhua/Photoshot), 6 (ZUMA Press), 33 (bottom) (ST1/HS1 WENN Photos), 41 (He Liu/Xinhua/Photoshot); Shutterstock pp. 9 (Andrey Shadrin), 17 (Tyler Olson), 20 (vso), 43 (Gabi Moisa), 45 (top) (saiko3p), 47 (Mordechai Meiri); Superstock pp. 20 (top left) (© imagebroker.net), 21 (© Science Faction).

Cover photograph of a woman wearing a sun hat reproduced with permission of Getty Images (Fuse). Cover logo reproduced with permission of Shutterstock (Olivier Le Moal).

Every effort has been made to contact copyright holders of material reproduced in this book. Any omissions will be rectified in subsequent printings if notice is given to the publisher.

Contents

Some words are shown in bold, **like this**. You can find out what they mean by looking in the glossary.

Important!

Please check with an adult before doing the projects in this book.

What is eco-fashion?

Eco-fashion, also known as earth-friendly fashion or **sustainable** clothing, is trendy and in vogue. Choosing **natural fibres** or **organically produced fabrics** is widespread. Taking responsibility for the environment and considering a garment's **carbon footprint** has become an important consideration for millions of shoppers.

In fact, wearing recycled or second-hand clothing has become fashionable. However, sustainable clothing seems to be more than a passing trend. As more people embrace eco-fashion for ethical or style reasons, it looks set to become part of most people's everyday lives.

Artists and fashion designers have found ways of making beautiful couture dresses using recycled copy paper, old photographs, books, and wrappers. By cutting, folding, hot gluing, and sewing paper, they are creating works of art to wear.

Responsible luxury

These days, top designers such as Vivienne Westwood, Stella McCartney, Donna Karan, and Ralph Lauren are working with eco-ideas and practices, too. Stella McCartney has always tried to source her materials ethically but it is only recently that she has publicized her eco-practices. In spring 2012, McCartney launched a new eco-friendly line of sunglasses. These shades were made from more than 50 per cent natural and renewable resources. Donna Karan has created T-shirts made from a blend of bamboo and **organic** cotton.

These models are wearing creations by designer Jeff Garner at Eco-Fashion Week in Vancouver, Canada.

Eco Impact

Bamboo is a fast-growing woody grass. It's a good sustainable material for clothes and household items such as furniture. Bamboo can grow up to 1 metre (3.28 feet) in one day!

The high street goes green

Some high street shops are also going green. Many retail clothing chains are increasing their use of organic cotton. A few shops have also experimented with recycled fibres. Meanwhile, some shops are looking at ways of encouraging their customers to recycle. In 2010, one major store attempted to up its eco-standards by giving its customers a big discount on a new pair of jeans when they donated their old denims to be recycled.

The green debate

Making the decision to be green is not really a big one. It isn't difficult. Some people say having a green wardrobe is going to cost them more money or it's too much hassle. However, chances are you are already greener than you think. You may already swap clothes with your mates or give your old clothes to charity. You've possibly raided your older siblings' or parents' cupboards and re-styled their clothes to fit you. Perhaps you're already into making your own gear. In this book, you'll find lots of other ways to get into the eco-fashion scene. You'll also discover how easy and rewarding being green is. Just knowing that you're doing your bit to preserve the planet for the future is one of the best feelings ever.

Livia Firth is one of the founders of the Eco Age shop in London. She's also the wife of Oscar-winning actor Colin Firth. Livia attends red carpet events wearing eco-clothes. She says, "For me, it's about trying to be a responsible consumer. It's about not being wasteful, buying less but better quality."

What's in it for the planet?

Choosing eco-fashion means:

- we waste fewer resources
- we save energy
- we reduce the amount of waste going to **landfill**
- we're helping other people
- we're reducing pollution
- we're respecting animals, people, and the environment.

What's in it for me?

- Reusing what you already have will cost you less.
- Re-invent your wardrobe and discover your own look. By shopping at charity shops and independent fashion stores, you'll be using your creativity and ingenuity. At the same time, you'll be creating a fantastic new look that you can't buy on the high street.
- You're going to have fun – you'll find out more about yourself and what you really like and believe in.
- Great green credentials may help you get the career you want in the future. Perhaps you're hankering after a job in fashion. Eco-fashion is more popular than ever, so by being green and learning how to shop responsibly you're gaining invaluable knowledge.
- The feel-good factor! You're taking charge of the situation and doing something to reduce your carbon footprint and save the planet.

This is an organic cotton plant. Going organic means reducing the use of **pesticides** and pollutants in farming. There are also major health benefits for cotton farmers. Non-organic cotton uses more pesticide per cotton plant than just about any other crop in the world. This can cause serious illness amongst farmers, and can also affect local eco-systems. Plants and animals can die as a result of exposure to pesticides.

Being eco

Some people follow the latest trends and wear things hot off the high street. Others create their own style and buy from charity shops. Today, many people have made the connection between the production of clothes and the impact on the environment. They choose eco-fashion or sustainable clothing. Hopefully, this book will show you how easy it is to be into eco-fashion.

The five Rs

You are going to hear a lot about the five Rs in this book. Most people already know about reduce, reuse, and recycle. Add "rethink" and "respect" to the list and we have all we need to tackle our wardrobes while making a real difference to the environment.

The big rethink

- *Rethink:* Are you a fast-fashion victim? Do you buy lots of cheap, low-quality, **mass-produced** clothes to keep up with the latest trends?

- *Reduce:* Being green means buying fewer new clothes. Do you really need five tops that look almost exactly the same?

- *Reuse:* Instead of throwing out unwanted clothes, you could think about how you can alter them or accessorize them to look different.

- *Recycle:* One person's rubbish is another's treasure. Giving unwanted gear to friends or charity is good for you, them, and the planet.

- *Respect:* If you look after your things they will last longer, which means you will consume less and reduce your carbon footprint. Another tip is to buy classic or timeless clothes that never go out of fashion.

Eco Impact

If every person in the United Kingdom bought one piece of recycled woollen clothing each year, it would save an average of 1,686 million litres (371 gallons) of water!

RETHINK
Little changes in my life can have a big impact on the environment.

REDUCE
Do I really need that new pair of shoes?

REUSE
I can dye old clothes to make them look like new.

RESPECT
Look after your gear and it can last a lifetime.

RECYCLE
Old clothes can be cut up to make scarves, bandanas, or belts.

THE BIG RETHINK

Counting the cost

Part of thinking green is trying to calculate the cost of each fashion item to the environment and society. Many people have a cheap white T-shirt, but what is the true cost of this simple item of clothing? Cotton production alone accounts for high volumes of pesticides and chemicals that pollute the environment. There is also a human cost because many T-shirts are produced in economically underdeveloped countries. In Bangladesh, for example, many garment workers spend 12 hours a day working in dangerous, cramped conditions for lower than average wages.

Make a snazzy top

Take one old T-shirt, grab some scissors, and fashion your very own gorgeous slinky slitted top!

You will need:

Big T-shirt
Sharp scissors
Tailor's chalk
Thick masking tape

Tailor's chalk is a hard chalk that leaves a temporary mark on clothes. Ordinary chalk or a machine washable felt-tip pen could be used instead.

Method:

1. Lay the T-shirt on a flat surface with the front facing upwards. Mark out the cut lines using tailor's chalk to match the template on the right.

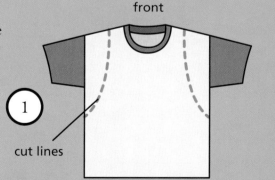

front

1

cut lines

2. Turn the T-shirt over and mark the cut lines on the back using tailor's chalk. Make sure the cut lines on the back and front join up at the sides.

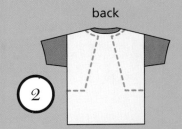

3. Cut out the basic shape of the T-shirt using the cut lines as guides.

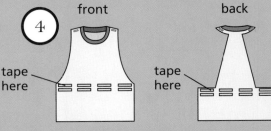

4. Use the masking tape to mark out where the waistband and shoulders will go.

5. Mark out cut lines on the front and back with chalk.

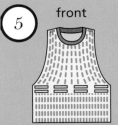

6. Now, cut along the lines. Remember to keep the cuts straight and parallel. Do not cut over the masking tape around the waistband or shoulder area.

7. Using these first cut lines as your guide, cut more parallel even lines along the front and back of the T-shirt to achieve the fringed look.

Inspirational ways with old tees

There are countless ways of getting more life out of old T-shirts. If they can't be used as garments, then give them away to charity. Or, cut them up and use them for dusters around the house. Here are some more creative ideas that are simple and effective:

- Turn an old T-shirt into a bag. All you need to do is cut off the sleeves and neckline of the T-shirt. Then, sew up the bottom hem and along the top, and add straps.

- Create a funky cushion cover. Cut off the sleeves and neckline of a T-shirt. Sew along the bottom hem. Place a cushion inside and sew along the top seam. This obviously works well if your T-shirt has a good design or picture on it.

- Re-fashion T-shirts you don't wear any more. Cut off the sleeves and neckline for an instant change. There are also plenty of ideas online about how you can make a halter neck T-shirt or a shrug by cutting down your unwanted T-shirts.

- An old T-shirt is great for dressing up. You can turn a plain T-shirt into almost any fancy-dress costume. Splatter a white tee with fake blood at Halloween. Get out the fabric paints and paint on the chain mail armour and coat of arms for a medieval knight. Cut up an old T-shirt to make a tunic for a Roman centurion.

Poppy - fashion angel

Poppy is a teenager and has her own blog about fashion:

"I can't afford to buy all the new up and coming clothes because I can't earn any money at my age so 'make do and mend' is something I like to keep in mind. Once, instead of spending my money on a new watch I dug out an old watch that my Grandma gave to me to play 'dress-up'. I just changed the battery et *voila*, a new watch – bargain! I also love buying, altering, and wearing second-hand items because nobody else has the same things and they can't just go out and copy me."

The eco answer

You've seen how easy it is to do something fun with your unwanted T-shirts on pages 10–11. This may be the beginning of a small business venture or valuable work experience. In this book, you'll find many more creative ideas and ways you can help the environment.

By opting for eco-clothing, you'll be helping the environment and will feel better about yourself. Confidence isn't something you wear, but it's a good look!

Being green - summing up

- Remember: Rethink, Reduce, Reuse, Recycle, and Respect.
- Be aware of the cost of your clothes to the environment.
- Look at your unwanted clothes in a new way – they are valuable and could have new life in them.
- Being green means shopping green. Look for timeless clothes that you will wear for years.
- Forget fast fashion or fad fashion.

Being green in action

Most teenagers love to shop for clothes. A day out browsing at a shopping centre is a popular pastime. Part of the appeal is finding the most recent fashions at affordable prices. Bagging a bargain has become a thrill in itself. These days, many more of us are filling up our virtual trolleys and checking out online because it's easy and cheaper than the high street shops. Not everyone has access to the web but they can use catalogues or order from magazines. We are surrounded by so much choice and ways in which to shop that it can be hard to resist buying into the fashion scene. This is "fast fashion" – fashion when we want it.

Some fashion journalists are telling us that "green is the new black". It's great to be fashionable, but it feels even better if you make choices that benefit the environment.

The fast fashion dilemma

When we do buy into the latest trends, we may not be making the wisest choices for the environment. Part of being eco is thinking about how we shop. It's about taking responsibility for the choices that we make and remembering the impact our fashion fixes have on the environment. One way to revolutionize the way you shop is to stop and think about fast fashion.

Fast fashion debate

Pros

- It's cheap. You can buy a dress for less than a large coffee.
- Low prices mean more people can afford the latest fashions.
- It's interesting and fun to move with the times.

Cons

- Fast fashion is seen as **disposable**. This is wasteful and bad for the environment.
- Cheap clothes have to be produced by somebody in a factory somewhere in the world. What are conditions and pay like for those workers?
- Fast fashion means people don't think about what they buy and wear. They often end up looking like everyone else.
- It costs nothing at all to reuse the clothes you already have.

Can you think of any more arguments for and against fast fashion?

Workers in clothing factories in Bangladesh work from 7 a.m. till 10 p.m., often seven days a week. They earn only about £12 a month. Young children often work in these terrible conditions.

New shopping habits

The decision not to buy fast fashion will mean changes to your shopping habits. Here's a useful "go green" shopping list:

Shopping list

- Shop around! You may be used to shopping at the same chains or have your favourite brands. Be prepared to change your ways and make an effort to find independent shops that make more effort to source green clothing.

- Go for clothes made from organic materials such as cotton, linen, jute, silk, ramie (a silky white natural fibre), and wood. Organic cotton (see page 7) is grown using fewer harmful pesticides and fewer harmful chemicals are used in its production.

- Where possible, choose clothes made from recycled materials because this uses less energy. Remember, the energy we use has an impact on climate change!

- Look out for quality gear that is going to last a long time. Over time, this reduces the amount of energy used for clothes production.

- Think about how the garment was made. If it's hand-knitted using local wool then you are benefiting the environment by reducing resources used for transporting goods. It's good practice to cut out transportation by air, reducing **air miles**, where possible.

- Slow down and take time to ask questions about what you're buying. Lots of savvy eco-shoppers want to buy fairly-traded items. Many retailers are happy to talk about the goods on sale, from where they came, and how they were made.

- Remember that you can always refuse to buy something. If you do decide not to buy an item on ethical grounds, tell the retailer why you have made that decision.

Check the label

Appearances can be deceptive. Always look carefully at the labels on any item of clothing or accessory you wish to buy. Read the care labels and other "eco-labels" and make informed choices.

- Check out the washing instructions on the garments and follow them. Delicates and woollens often need to be hand-washed. Stick to the recommendations if you want your clothes to last.
- Try to steer clear of clothes that need to be dry-cleaned. The dry cleaning process uses harmful chemicals which can be bad for people and pollute the environment.
- Wise up to the eco-labels on the things you buy. Labels to look out for include the EU Eco Label and the Oeko-Tex Standard 100. The Oeko-Tex Standard 100 is an international label. It lets you know that the textile or item of clothing doesn't contain chemicals that can harm human health (see page 20).

Eco-shoppers say "no" to fast fashion. They also slow down and think about what they are buying. Don't be embarrassed to look at the labels on clothes, and to ask questions, too.

Feel the quality – will it stand the test of time?

Check the care label.

Look at the label to find out what the garment is made from.

Respect

Eco-fashion is about respecting human life, animal life, and plant life. That's why many eco-fashion stores have a fair trade policy or strive towards making ethically-produced goods. Designers that believe in animal rights do not use any animal products. Likewise, many companies have a zero waste policy, which means that they reuse or recycle all products used in all parts of their business.

The International FAIRTRADE Certification Mark is there to show you that producers in the developing world are getting fair pay and working in good conditions. The Fairtrade mark is certified by an independent organization so you can always trust it. Some countries, such as the USA, use slightly different marks, but as long as they are genuine, they mean the same thing. See www.fairtrade.net for more information.

Purchase power

Fashion can be an individual statement of who you are and what you believe. For example, in the 1960s many people grew their hair long and wore unconventional clothing to show they were part of the hippie movement and embraced its ideas about peace, love, and freedom. In the same way, young black people in the 1990s sometimes expressed their feelings of being marginalized within wider society by wearing clothes influenced by hip-hop culture.

These days we can choose clothes that express our views about the environment, animal rights, and **Fairtrade**, too. Not too long ago, a vegan would have had a limited choice of ethical footwear from which to choose. Now, funky vegan footwear (shoes made without any animal products) is readily up for grabs. In the same way, a person who believes passionately in decent pay and conditions for producers will be able to source clothes that have been fairly traded – it just so happens that many of these businesses are eco, too!

Fashion can be both ethical and exciting. The EDUN ready-to-wear spring collection of 2012 got the fashion press talking.

Style with substance

One of the pioneers of ethical clothing is the brand EDUN. Launched in 2005 by rock star Bono and his wife Ali Hewson, EDUN aims to create a global fashion brand focusing on trade with Africa and other developing countries. In 2007, EDUN launched EDUN Live, a division committed to producing T-shirts that are 100 per cent grown and sewn in Africa.

Part of EDUN's philosophy is ensuring that all its factories comply with legal labour and health and safety regulations to promote good working conditions. In 2007, EDUN joined forces with the Wildlife Conservation Society to form the Conservation Cotton Initiative. The programme promotes the production of eco-friendly cotton farming.

Greenwashing

Watch out for "**greenwashing**". Some fashion companies use clever marketing to make their products sound eco-friendly. In short, don't always trust what you read on the label or advertising material. Just because a company uses a natural fabric in its collections doesn't mean to say that they are "green". Such companies may use harmful chemicals such as bleach or dyes in the production process.

Look closely at the labelling and check the item has been produced using **natural dyes**. Likewise, check that **synthetic** materials haven't been added to "organic" clothes. It isn't just the fabric in question here – it's the buttons, zips, and other accessories. If it isn't on the label and there's any doubt, then you always have the option not to buy.

Which are the genuine eco-labels?

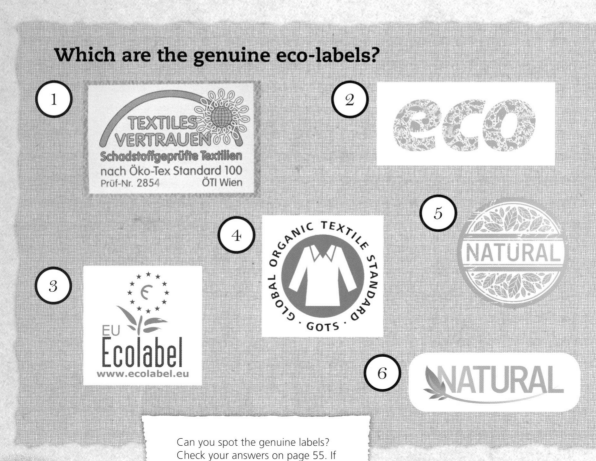

Can you spot the genuine labels? Check your answers on page 55. If you want to see more genuine eco-labels from around the world visit: www.ecolabelindex.com/ecolabels.

Synthetic fabric dyes are not environmentally friendly. The dying process uses lots of water and produces pollution. The dyes can also cause health problems. Look for clothes that use natural dyes – or that haven't been dyed at all.

Green transport

Other things to remember when you shop for eco-fashion include low-impact shipping of goods. Low-impact shipping is about transporting goods in a way that has little impact on the environment. Increasing emissions from transport poses a serious threat to the environment. If this is something that concerns you, then there are fashion retailers who are trying to use low-impact shipping. You can always shop around until you find a company that offers this service.

Eco-packaging

Another consideration is eco-packaging. Now that more people are shopping online, there is greater need for packaging. These days, there are ranges of **biodegradable** mailing bags and specialist recycled paper which help to make posting items more environmentally friendly. There are plenty of retailers who can help you with eco-packaging. Finally, don't forget to keep and reuse the packaging used by clothing companies.

Bags of choice

We are often encouraged to reuse plastic carrier bags, purchase "bags for life", or use our own eco-friendly canvas or cotton shopping bags. There's a good reason for this: many plastic bags don't easily decompose in landfill. In fact, it takes *thousands of years* for them to fully decompose. When they finally do, they will pollute the soil and water. While biodegradable plastic carrier bags are available, they do not have the green credentials of a reusable canvas bag!

Second-hand shopping

Another green choice is to buy second-hand from charity shops. You can find fantastic one-off items or some prize vintage garments at a snip of the cost they'd be to buy new in the shops. You'll also be able to indulge in some guilt-free shopping safe in the knowledge that you're reusing clothes and possibly rescuing them from landfill.

Second-hand clothes can be a fast-track to cool. Retro-style shirts are all the rage on the high street, but you may find something unique in a second-hand stall or street market.

The problems with synthetics

Did you know that many man-made fabrics are not eco-friendly? Traditional synthetic fabrics such as polyester or nylon are made from petrochemicals, derived from crude oil and natural gas. Not only is their production energy-intensive but large amounts of water are required for cooling. These fabrics do not biodegrade, either.

To dispose of them, give them away to charity, sell them on, or make sure the fabric is recycled and used again. Another consideration is that synthetic materials don't "breathe". They make people sweat more, and so need to be washed more regularly.

Jumble sale shopping

Why not organize an eco-jumble sale as a fundraising event at school? People can get rid of the clothes they don't want anymore in a responsible way. At the jumble sale, they may be able to grab themselves a few bargains and go home with some new gear they love. In the process, some money is raised for charity or for another good cause.

When you shop at jumble sales, markets, and charity shops, you may discover some hilarious old styles, as well as find an absolute bargain.

Being green - summing up

- Discover new shops and retail outlets with greener clothes.
- Buy only what you really need.
- Choose clothes made from natural, sustainable fabrics.
- Be aware of greenwashing.
- Use paper or reusable bags. Ask about eco-friendly packing and wrapping, and opt for low-impact shipping.
- Buy green to show your support for eco-friendly production processes.

Reuse and rejoice!

When it comes to fashion, there's a fine line between reuse and recycle. In this chapter, we'll look at simple ways that you can reuse many old clothes or fabrics that you might normally chuck away. First of all, you need to take a long, hard look at the clothes, shoes, accessories, and jewellery that you do have. Sort them into piles: keep, revive, give away or swap, sell, or charity shop. There's also bound to be a pile of clothes you can't see a need for – there will be some cunning ideas for those later! Take your time over the process and do it one step at a time.

By reusing your old clothes, you may come up with some fabulous new looks. Experiment with mixing smart and casual styles. For example, a hardly-worn waistcoat could look great with a pair of your old jeans.

Eco Impact

Some textiles might not be biodegradable but almost 100 per cent are suitable for recycling or reuse. There are hundreds of potential uses for recycled textiles. Shredded fabric can be used as furniture padding, mattresses, thermal insulation, and roofing felts.

By reducing textile waste we can *reduce* landfill, *reduce* energy used to get rid of waste, and *reduce* emissions of poisonous polluting gases into the atmosphere.

A few simple badges can transform a suit jacket. This is another look that works well with jeans and a T-shirt.

Wardrobe revamp

Once you have sorted your clothes and accessories into piles, take a look at what you have decided to revive. These items may not be that old, but might feel dated or over-familiar. With a little time and imagination, you can find ways to make them last a few more seasons. Here are a few simple tricks that will save you money and help the environment:

- Add a belt to make a dress, top, jumper, or jacket look completely different.
- Change the buttons of a top or cardigan for an instant make-over.
- Transform your outfit by accessorizing with pom poms, bows, fake flowers, scarves, and jewellery.
- Change or add a new collar to a jacket. Perhaps you could add a strip of fake fur or lace to a collar for a whole new look.
- Get out the scissors and chop the bottoms off old or ripped jeans. Cut them to around knee length so you can wear them in the summer.
- Dying clothes or shoes is an easy way to keep up with the season's colours. Buy cold dyes and transform old clothes in your kitchen. Use natural dyes so you won't be polluting the planet, either.

Jeans made good

Jeans are a staple in many people's wardrobes. However, certain styles seem to come and go each season. Perhaps fashion fads don't bother you and you prefer classic styles anyway. However, if following fashion is for you then hang on to jeans that haven't been worn out. Chances are that skinny, bootleg, or flared jeans will all come back into fashion one day. Meanwhile, the fashion for ripped jeans also comes and goes. You can always buy distressed or ripped jeans but it's incredibly easy to customize your own.

Customize your jeans

You will need:

A clean pair of jeans – these can be jeans you already have or buy
  a cheap pair from a charity shop.
Scissors
Ruler
Tailor's chalk or pen
Coarse sandpaper, pumice stone, wood file, or grater
Utility knife
Block of wood to cut on (it should be able to fit inside the trouser leg)
Environmentally friendly bleach

Method:

1. Decide where you want to have a rip or where you would like the jeans to look distressed. Avoid putting the rips too close together.

2. Draw a line on the jeans using the ruler and tailor's chalk or pen.

3. Place the block of wood under the line.

4. Rub along the line with the sand paper, pumice stone, or wood file. Try rubbing in different directions. You may get the distressed effect you like just by rubbing.

5. To get a full rip, you may need to use the utility knife or scissors.

6. Remember each time you wash the jeans they will get more distressed and frayed.

"Make do and mend"

Reusing old clothes isn't a new thing! "Make do and mend" was an idea introduced to Britain during World War II. All resources, including textiles, were restricted or rationed. People were encouraged to reuse their old clothes by darning and fixing them. They were also shown how to alter necklines or nip in waists to change the look of clothes.

Adult clothes were cut down and reused by children. Some brides wore dresses made from silk parachutes. People kept and reused everything, including old zips, bits of old ribbon, buttons, hooks and eyes, and they even unravelled the wool from jumpers to be used again. There were restrictions on some clothes and shoes in the United States, too. People learned how to improvise and make the most of their clothes. Sometimes this created a whole new fashion.

Dream dresses

Prom dresses, evening gowns, or bridesmaid dresses are a "make do and mend" dream. There are so many things to do with an elaborate frock. Rather than let it hang in the back of your wardrobe, the dress can be put to good use for you or others.

Some girls can't afford to splash out on an expensive evening dress. Several organizations have found a way round the problem. They collect hardly-worn dresses and give them away to girls who can't afford a new dress. Giving to charity or thrift shops is another option.

Here are some ideas for revamping your dress:

- Transform a full-skirted gown into a princess dress to wear at a fancy dress party.
- If you don't want to wear the dress again, make it into a gift for someone else. With time, imagination, and a few snips and stitches it could be a charming frock for a little girl.
- Restyle the dress so it could be worn at another dressy occasion. For example, you could shorten it to wear to a wedding or party.
- Could you make a separate skirt and top? Or, alter the length of the skirt and redo the sleeves and neckline of the top half.
- Whatever you decide to do with your gown, remember to keep the material you cut off. This can be used to make scarves, hair ties, bands, or belts.

Have a look at the suggestions on the next page, too.

Swap-O-Rama-Rama

Swap-O-Rama-Rama organizes events guaranteed to get you into clothes swapping and creative reuse of clothing. The idea is that participants turn up at the event with a bag of their unwanted clothes. First, they swap their gear. Next, they work at various DIY stations learning how to alter clothes, add appliqué, or even how to do silk screen printing. Everyone goes home with a bag of free clothes and lots of inspiration ideas. The Swap-O-Rama-Rama network began in New York, USA, and now takes place in over 100 cities all round the world.

Revamp an old frock

original dress

You could wear your dress to another smart occasion by removing the straps and cutting away a few ruffles from the hem.

You could wear the top of the dress anywhere if you pair it with jeans and a wide leather belt.

Re-use the skirt from the dress. Team your fancy skirt with a plain top. To get a more edgy look, wear boots and accessorise with wristbands or other chunky jewellery.

29

Swap shop

Let's go back to those piles of clothes and accessories you made at the beginning of the chapter. Next, look at the pile you thought about giving away or swapping. Most people make impulse buys in sales or never get round to taking things back to the shop. However, we can all learn by our mistakes so make a note to yourself not to act on impulse and waste money in the future!

Chances are you already give away these mistakes or swap them with your friends. There are also internet sites devoted to swapping unwanted clothes. Swapping is great because you get all the thrill of getting something new without spending any money.

Party party

Clothes swap parties are getting more popular. This is a great way to socialize and if you follow these simple instructions then everyone should go home happy...

How to host a clothes swap party

Planning ahead

1. Make sure there's a venue you can use. Ask permission if you want to host the party at your house.

2. Set a date for the party a few weeks in advance. This gives everyone time to sort through their wardrobe and find the clothes they want to swap.

3. Think about who you want to invite. It makes sense to invite people who have the same tastes and sizes in clothes or people of a similar age.

4. Don't invite too many people – you don't want people falling over each other to get to the clothes!

5. Make invitations. These should include the date, time, and venue. Give instructions to wash clothes for the swap and how many items to bring. If this is a fundraising event, add the entrance fee. Finally, decide whether people should bring the gear on the night or in advance.

The party!

- Arrange things so they are easy to find. Place similar items together. Use a clothes rail for dresses and coats. Another fun idea is to let people model some of the clothes.

- Remember this is going to be a party so provide food, drinks, and music.

- Let people take it in turns to choose an item. People may want the same thing so be prepared to settle any disagreements.

Eva and Matilda's Clothes Swap Party

Matilda's house: 13 Pear Tree Lane

Saturday, 29th March

7pm, free entrance

Bring 5 clean garments to Matilda's house by 22nd March.
They will be sorted and ready to swap for
5 new items on the big night.

Thrifty and nifty

If you can't swap or exchange your gear, donating to charity shops is an excellent eco-alternative. Many shops make an effort to hang clothes so people can find what they're looking for. Young fashion lines are often hung together on rails. If you give your clothes away to charity, you'll not only be helping the environment but you will be helping out those who are less fortunate.

The Freecycle way

There are lots of other ways to give your clothes away. The Freecycle Network began in Arizona, USA, in 2003. The project began when a group of citizens in Tucson grouped together to find a way of redistributing their unwanted goods (anything from washing machines to woollen mittens) and saving them from landfill. The idea was to match people who had things to give away or recycle with people who needed them.

Now there are Freecycle groups all over the world in an estimated 85 countries. The concept works well with clothes, too. If a person has something to offer, such as a bag of children's clothes or a brand new ski jacket, then they email the group. Likewise, if somebody wants something, such as an evening gown or wedding suit, then they circulate a message to the group.

Be safe!

Meeting people online obviously poses risks to your safety. Make sure you get the help of a parent or other responsible adult when you look for Freecycle groups near you. Always ensure that there is an adult around when an item is dropped off or picked up.

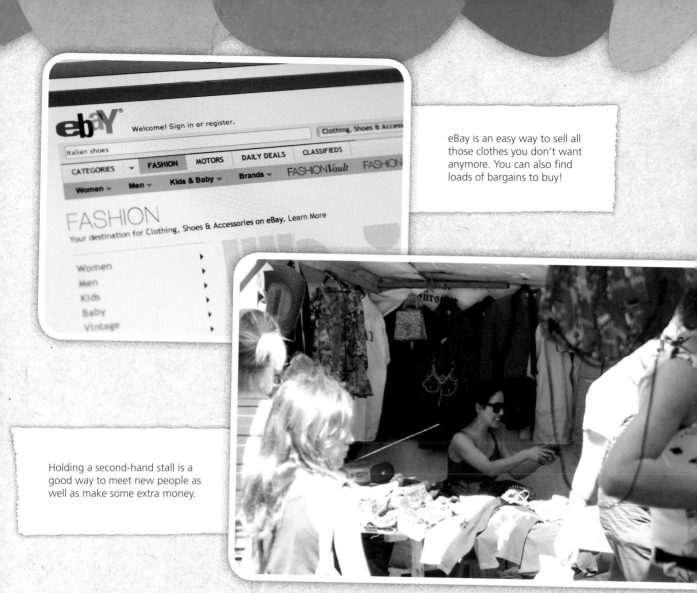

eBay is an easy way to sell all those clothes you don't want anymore. You can also find loads of bargains to buy!

Holding a second-hand stall is a good way to meet new people as well as make some extra money.

Ways to make money

There are lots of ways to make money from your unwanted clothes:

- Have a garage sale or junk sale. This is a way of raising money by selling all your unwanted household goods as well as clothes. They usually take place in the garage, front garden, or driveway of your home.
- Sell at a car boot sale. Fill the boot of your parents' car with all those fashion items you don't want anymore.
- Sell to a second-hand, vintage, resale, or consignment shop. Scout around before you sell, to make sure you are going to the best shop.
- Organize a second-hand clothing stall at your next school fête, fair, or other fund-raising event.
- Sell your gear on internet auction sites like eBay.

A new life – cool sweatshirts

Getting back to that pile of things you don't want any more, and don't think anybody else will either. You could try turning your old things into something new and exciting. Most people have a couple of sweatshirts they don't wear any more. Tie-dying is an easy and effective way of making the most of that boring old top that has seen better days. There are all kinds of ways of creating the tie-dyed effect. For the following project, elastic bands are used.

How to tie-dye a sweatshirt

You will need:

A sweatshirt (preferably light coloured)
Cold water dye
Salt
Elastic bands

Method:

1. Lay the sweatshirt out flat on a smooth surface.

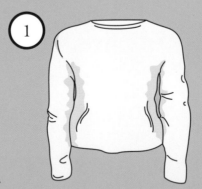

2. Concertina-fold the sweatshirt so it's ready for dyeing. Start at the bottom edge. Fold the edge up about 5 cm (2 in). Turn the sweatshirt over and fold the edge down about 5 cm (2 in).

3. Continue concertina-folding until the top looks a folded paper fan.

4. Take a rubber band and wrap it tightly around the folded top about 4 cm (1½ in) away from one of the ends.

5. Continue to wrap rubber bands along the whole length about 4 cm (1½ in) apart.

6. The sweatshirt is now ready to be dyed. Read the instructions for using the dye carefully. Follow the instructions and timings and you should have a fantastic tie-dyed top!

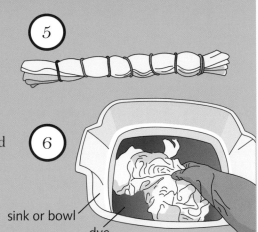

sink or bowl

dye

DIY jewellery

Gather all the bits of jewellery you have – even if a piece is out of date or broken – and think about how you could make a new piece. Could all those beads be restrung on to a piece of cord or leather? Maybe you could make your own funky version of a charm bracelet. It's easy to buy new clips and other fittings at craft stores.

Remodelling and recycling jewellery

Jewellery designer Louise Hall has set up her own online jewellery business specializing in handmade and ethical jewellery. She works with reclaimed scraps such as X-ray and film plates, as well as found objects. Louise has also set up a jewellery recycling service. Customers can send her all their unwanted jewellery and she can either remodel these bits into something new or she can offer the customer cash.

The revamp camp – new trainers

This chapter has been all about taking stock and working with the fashion items you already own. The benefit to you is you'll be saving cash and re-inventing your wardrobe. You'll also benefit the environment by reducing your carbon footprint. Try this idea to give an old pair of shoes the make-over they've been waiting for…

Make some snazzy cartoon trainers

You will need:

Old shoes
Scissors
All-in-one glue, sealer, and finish
Paintbrush
Comics

Method:

1. Cut up the cartoon strip into small sections that will fit on to the shoe. Keep all the bits you cut away to use later.

2. Work on one area of the shoe at a time. Use the paintbrush to apply the all-in-one glue, sealer, and finish to one side of one shoe.

3. Apply a strip of comic on to the shoe over the glue. Smooth it with your fingers to make sure there are no wrinkles. You may need to cut off parts of the comic as you go to make it fit the shoe properly.

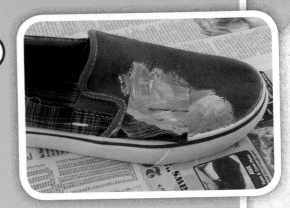

4. Repeat until you have covered the whole shoe.

5. There may be small gaps between the comic strips. Apply thin strips of glue to these areas and fill them in with the little pieces of comic you cut off earlier.

6. Cut off any comic that is hanging over the bottom edge of the shoe. Aim to create a straight line along the bottom edge where the upper shoe meets the sole.

7. Once you are satisfied with how the shoe looks, paint the all-in-one glue, sealer, and finish all over the shoe. This will seal the comics to the shoe and make it look shiny.

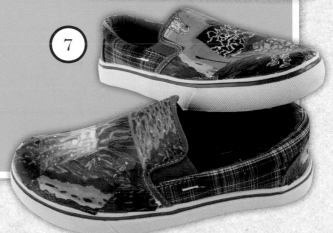

8. Let the glue dry fully before you wear them.

Being green - summing up

- Look after the clothes you keep.
- Use your imagination to restyle old clothes.
- Swap unwanted clothes with friends and family.
- Give your old clothes to charity or sell them to make a profit.
- Buy new clothes made from natural, sustainable fabrics.

Recycle, recycle

Once you've done the big blitz on your wardrobe and sorted everything out there may be a pile of things that are too worn for anything. This is where the next part of the green journey begins. This is when discarded items go down the recycling route.

Reuse versus recycle

By giving your unwanted clothes to charity shops or placing them in recycling banks you are ensuring many of your items will be recycled. Clothing sent to charity shops or placed in textile recycling banks is generally sorted into categories:

1. Better quality clothes are often exported. They are sent to poorer countries especially in Africa and Eastern Europe. (REUSE)
2. Damaged, worn out gear is often sold as rags – to be used as clothes or mattress filling, for example. (REUSE)
3. Other worn out fabric is cleaned, shredded, and converted into recycled fibre called shoddy. (RECYCLE)
4. The remaining items are scrapped and sent to landfill or incinerated. (SCRAP)

Recycling bins are usually colour-coded or clearly marked so you know what to put where. In some places, there are even pink bins for recycling old bras.

Recycled fabric

Natural fabrics such as cotton and silk and synthetic fabrics such as polyester and rayon are all recyclable. At **reclamation mills**, old garments are sorted into type and colour and then stripped of buttons and zips. Different fabrics undergo different processes. In general, the recycled material is converted back into fibres. This is spun and woven into fabric that can be used again. Anything from bags to brand new T-shirts can be made using recycled fabric.

The chain H&M introduced the Conscious Collection in 2012. The environmentally friendly collection uses recycled materials and organic cotton.

Plastic fashion

Did you know that recycled bottles are used to make fleeces, T-shirts, and baseball caps? It's hard to believe, but synthetic fleece is made from polyester, which is spun plastic. Repreve is the trade name of a new kind of polyester made from 100 per cent recycled fibres. No newly refined oil is required. The process also uses less energy and water, and produces fewer greenhouse gas emissions than making brand new (virgin) synthetic fibres.

Fun with eco-fashion

Recycled or restyled clothing is all the rage. This is taking vintage or second-hand clothes and reconstructing them into new and exciting contemporary pieces of clothing. Some fashion designers have been having fun with the concept for years. They have mixed and matched different garments to create some truly one-off numbers.

Take the plunge

You don't have to be good at sewing to create recycled clothes but it does help. Just as important is having imagination and a good eye. This means looking at old or discarded clothes and dreaming up or sketching ways of how they can be reborn. Ask your family if you can look through their wardrobes. You may find some garments in your parents' wardrobes that are out of fashion or too big but have huge potential because they are made from quality material or the fabric has a funky design. You may find male suits that could make the basis of a sassy suit for a young woman. Remember that any item is a sum of its parts. You may not like the skirt or top of a dress but could part of it be used successfully again? Perhaps one dress has a beautiful belt or buttons that you could add to another dress you have in mind. Let your imagination go wild and enjoy yourself.

Hats off to this eco-fashion designer's latest creation. By reusing lots of old fabric, something unique has been made.

This 2011 show in Cali, Columbia was held by fashion students to display their eco designs. Everything on the catwalk was made from recycled materials.

An eco-fashion challenge

- Take a trip to a local charity shop or look through friends' and family's wardrobes.
- Select two or three garments that catch your eye. Think about how you could deconstruct them and turn them into an eye-catching garment that you would be proud to wear or give away.
- Sketch your ideas. Don't limit yourself to one design. Play around with your designs until you have something that is achievable and looks good.
- Take the plunge. Get to work with scissors, sewing machine, or needle and thread!

Being green - summing up

- Make sure unusable clothes enter the recycling system.
- Buy clothes made from recycled fabrics or recycled plastic.
- Don't throw anything away! Start a collection of buttons, zips, fabric, and ribbon to use later.
- Make or buy re-styled or recycled clothes.

The care cycle

Looking after your clothes helps to care for the environment. Rule number one is to buy the best quality you can afford. Higher quality not only lasts longer but survives the rigours of wearing, washing, drying, and ironing.

To wash or not to wash

A hot wash plays havoc with your clothes. Colours fade and sometimes clothes shrink or wear out more quickly. Hot washes also use more energy and water. Take time to think about your washing. Underwear and socks obviously need regular washes. But do jumpers, shirts, T-shirts, and jeans need to be washed after a single wear? Small marks can be sponged off. If you're really unsure whether your clothes can handle another outing, then do a quick smell check. If the armpit of your shirt doesn't smell, you can probably wear it again. Another trick is to hang up clothes that have been worn once outside for a blast of fresh air.

Some stained articles need to be washed at 40 degrees to get rid of allergens and clean them properly.

Wash well

If you love your clothes then wash them well. Here are a few ways to get the best out of a wash:

- Follow care labels to avoid shrinking or ruining your clothes.
- Wash whites, coloureds, and delicates separately.
- Turn delicates inside out or put them in a pillow case … OR
- …Wash delicates by hand.
- Use environmentally-friendly detergents or eco laundry balls.
- Opt for cool washes – 30 degrees – to cut costs and energy use.
- Wait until you have a full load before you do a wash.

A cool wash at 30 degrees will prevent wear and tear, and save energy and costs.

Use washing balls and eco-friendly detergents.

A full load of washing saves energy.

Eco Impact

Between 85 and 90 per cent of the energy used by a washing machine is for heating the water. One washing powder manufacturer suggests that over one year, washing at 30°C instead of 60°C saves enough carbon dioxide to fill 4 million double-decker buses. So, unless your clothes really do need a hot wash, manually set a 30°C economy wash!

Washday: dos and don'ts

Another way to avoid a hot wash is to pre-treat your clothes. This may mean pre-soaking them in a bucket of water with eco-friendly detergent or a tablespoon of borax (a washing agent that can be bought at household and hardware shops). Some stains may need a spot stain remover. There are plenty of natural stain-buster recipes you can make yourself using simple ingredients. These eco-friendly stain removers are less harmful to you and the environment.

Different kinds of stains need different treatments. However, the advice for treating all stains is the same:

- Act quickly before the stain has time to set.
- Cold water is the best treatment to begin with. Hot water can cause certain stains, such as blood, to set.
- Dab, don't rub, the stained fabric.
- Work at the stain from the inside and move outwards.

Dab, don't rub! Rubbing will set the stain and make it even harder to remove.

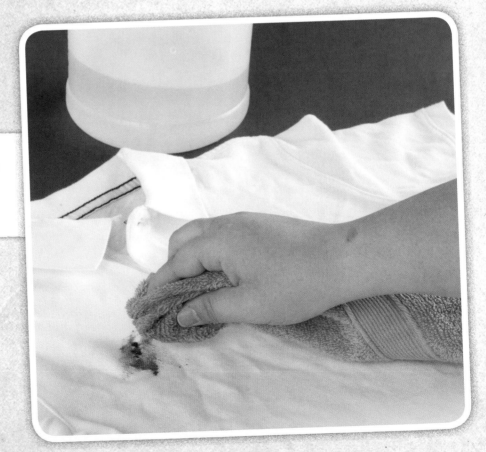

Quick and easy stain busters

- Egg and bloodstains respond well to a soak in salted water before washing.
- Chocolate stains can be treated in lukewarm soapy water. If this doesn't work, try soaking in glycerine (a commonly used liquid found at chemists and household stores) for 30 minutes before washing.
- Tea, coffee, red wine, or berry juices can be treated with lemon juice or white vinegar before going in the wash.
- Greasy stains such as butter, mayonnaise, oil, make-up, or candle wax can be pre-treated with a home-made paste of bicarbonate of soda and water.
- Lipstick and other make-up stains do well soaked in eucalyptus oil (a natural oil that can be purchased online or at the chemist) before laundering.
- Sweat stains can be soaked in water with 1–2 tablespoons of white vinegar or lemon juice or a handful of bicarbonate of soda before washing.

Dryer ideas

Tumble dryers are one of the most energy-hungry appliances in the home. By cutting back on using the tumble dryer, you could dramatically cut your household's carbon footprint. When the weather is fine, you can hang your washing outdoors on a line if you have space – your washing will smell great! Another tip is to add half a cup of lemon juice to the final rinse of a white wash. Lemon acts as a mild, environmentally-friendly bleach. If you dry the whites outdoors in full sun, they will naturally whiten as they dry. When the weather isn't so good, hang everything on clothes racks. Remember to give them a good shake first to avoid creases.

Did you know that an iron uses as much electricity as 18 light bulbs?

A stitch in time

In the past, people often said "a stitch in time saves nine", or did their best to "make do and mend". These are lessons we could all learn now. But a more modern and eco-friendly approach might be "repair not replace"! This means paying attention to those running repairs that clothes often need. In most cases, it pays to do the job quickly before the garment is damaged. A repair hit list may include:

- A button that needs replacing – hang on to buttons that fall off your clothes and keep them safe.
- A hem that needs to be taken up – do this before the hem gets frayed or damaged when it catches the floor.
- A seam that has come undone – stitch it up before the whole seam falls apart and frays.
- A small rip, tear, or hole – catch it quick before it becomes bigger!
- Patch up holes on the knees of trousers or elbows of tops. Keep interesting scraps of material to use as patches.

Keeping on top of these jobs makes your clothes last longer and costs you less.

This look is easy to achieve if you use sew-on patches.

Problem Prevention Plans

Don't forget PPP – Problem Prevention Plans. This means taking a few simple steps to protect your clothes.

Wear layers of clothing, especially underwear such as slips and vests, to protect garments from sweat stains and wear and tear. Or, layer up with T-shirts.

Cleaning and polishing your footwear will make it last longer. But many shoe polishes, conditioners, and protectors are expensive and filled with chemicals. Below is a list of alternatives (test them on a small spot first):

- Leather shoes can be rubbed with the inside of a banana peel, then buffed and shined with a soft rag.
- Olive oil conditions and shines smooth leather shoes.
- Rub a small amount of toothpaste on stained leather shoes and leave on for nine hours before buffing and shining.

Dirty canvas trainers can be washed in the machine.

Being green – summing up

- Avoid hot washes.
- Use eco-friendly washing products.
- Try natural stain-busting techniques.
- Hang your clothes outside to dry.
- Repair not replace.
- Think PPP – Problem Prevention Plans!

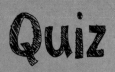

Quiz

Hopefully, this book has given you plenty of ideas about making sure your wardrobe is eco friendly. But how eco are you now? This quiz will help you find out where you're at and how you're going to plan your future. See page 50 to find out how you did.

1. **How often do you go clothes shopping?**
   a) I go shopping every week and usually come home with something new.
   b) About once a month. I like to save up and buy things that I really want.
   c) I only get things when I need them. If my shoes can't be repaired anymore then I will buy a new pair.

2. **Where/how do you shop for clothes?**
   a) Mostly on the high street. I can't resist a bargain and there are shops in town that have the latest looks for next to nothing.
   b) I like to shop around for my clothes to make sure I get what I really want. I do a lot of window-shopping but go online to see if I can find things cheaper.
   c) These days I go to the shops or online retailers that I know stock ethically-produced goods.

3. **Do you buy eco-friendly clothes?**
   a) I'm not sure. I buy things because I like the look of them.
   b) I try to do my bit for the environment by buying second-hand clothes. I reckon I could do more though.
   c) I always check the label on everything I buy. I buy natural fabrics because they use fewer resources and are sustainable.

4. What do you do with the clothes you don't want anymore?

a) I do swap some of my clothes but anything I don't want anymore I chuck away.

b) I give my old clothes to charity.

c) I never throw anything away. If I can't reuse my clothes or wear them in a different way then I love to swap with my friends.

5. What would you do with a T-shirt with a hole in it?

a) Bin it!

b) Depends on the size of the hole. If I couldn't repair it and make it look good then I'd give it away or something.

c) Turn it into a cushion or make a shopping bag. If it's really beyond repair, I rip it up to make rags for polishing my shoes.

6. What would you do with a cheap white T-shirt that had chocolate stains down the front?

a) If it was a bad stain then I'd probably just bin the T-shirt.

b) Pop the T-shirt in a hot wash and hope for the best.

c) Treat the stain with lemon juice then wash it by hand. If the stain didn't go after a few attempts, I might dye the T-shirt another colour.

6. What do you do when a button falls off your jacket or cardigan?

a) I can't be bothered to sew it back on. In fact, I don't even know *how* to sew a button on.

b) Sometimes I get around to sewing it back on or I ask my mum to do it.

c) I replace it as soon as possible. I've got a stash of buttons in a jar so if I can't find the button, I'll look for something similar. Sometimes I decide to change all the buttons and give the top a whole new look.

Quiz answers

Mostly As:

Sounds like you are a fast fashion-addict. Now is the time to break unhealthy shopping habits. Your throwaway attitude is no credit to you and doesn't help the environment. Think about introducing some simple changes to your life to get a more individualistic and eco-friendly style. Remember the five Rs – rethink, respect, reuse, recycle, and reduce – and you won't go far wrong.

Mostly Bs:

You're doing your bit to help the environment. However, there's loads more you could do so don't get too complacent. You already shop around for your clothes but take it one step further and insist upon eco-friendly fabrics. Get out your needle and thread and experiment with reusing clothes. Be more imaginative and you'll be rewarded with a funky, greener wardrobe.

Mostly Cs:

Wow, the world needs more people like you! You think carefully about how to shop. You also know how to reuse your gear and about the importance of recycling. Well done! You consider the environment every step of the way. Keep it up and tell everyone about the importance of going green.

A 10-point action plan

If you scored As and Bs in the quiz, you could use this 10-point action plan to improve your eco-fashion impact:

1. Sort out your wardrobe
2. Send unwanted items off to charity shops
3. Accessorize and experiment with the clothes you keep
4. Swap clothes with friends and family
5. Shop less, think ethically and organically
6. Buy quality – it lasts longer
7. Look after your gear and wash it well
8. Make do and mend
9. Reuse your unwanted garments to make interesting gifts
10. Recycle old gear – it *can* be used again.

A bag for life!

If you want a shopping bag that is 100 per cent ethical, then look out for one of the many bags that makes some money for charity, too. In 2006, model and campaigner Lauren Bush designed a bag to benefit the United Nations World Food Programme's (WFP) School Feeding programme. The FEED bags are made from sustainable material and all the money paid for the bags goes straight to feeding starving children around the world. The FEED foundation says that buying one bag pays for 30 meals.

Get stitching!

The ultimate eco-fashionista makes their own gear. You can download patterns from the internet. Some of the patterns are free and many of them are easy to do.

Saving water

Conserve water by reusing any jeans that are just hanging unworn in your wardrobe. Around 14,500 litres (3,190 gallons) of water goes into the manufacture of a new pair of jeans. This is because huge amounts of water are used in cotton production.

Saving energy

Approximately 60 per cent of the energy used in the life cycle of a cotton T-shirt is related to washing and drying at high temperatures after it has been bought.

Saving more energy

Textile recycling requires less energy than any other type of recycling, and it does not create any new hazardous waste or harmful by-products.

Eco-fashionista

To be a true eco-fashionista means making recycling a way of life. It means discarding all plastics and other disposables responsibly, making sure they reach the recycling system.

Eco Impact

A "True Cost" T-shirt is not your average T-shirt. It has a strong message for us all. Available online, each eco-friendly T-shirt spells out the cost of production from farm to fashion. The front of each T-shirt carries the following information:

True Cost of One White Cotton T-shirt
Non-Organic, Foreign Made 200g/7oz
Water: 570 gallons (45% irrigation)
Energy: 8kWh (machines), 11 to 29 gallons fuel
Travel: 5,500 to 9,400+ miles
Emissions: No_x, SO_2, CO, CO_2, N_2O, volatile compounds
Toxins: 1–3 pesticides, diesel exhaust, heavy metals (dyes)
Child Labour: 17 countries, 50c/day
Buy Online: http://true-cost.re-configure.org

Smelly trainers

Even smelly old trainers can be recycled and used again. Old trainers can be cut up and ground down to make surfaces for sports and playgrounds. Good news, when you consider how many of us wear trainers, and that they are impossible to biodegrade!